Lives
of the Artists

Claude
MONET

Lives
of the Artists

Claude
MONET

WORLD ALMANAC® LIBRARY

Please visit our web site at:
www.worldalmanaclibrary.com
For a free color catalog describing World Almanac®
Library's list of high-quality books and multimedia
programs, call 1-800-848-2928 (USA) or 1-800-387-3178
(Canada). World Almanac® Library's fax: (414) 332-3567.

Library of Congress Cataloging-in-Publication Data available upon request
from publisher. Fax (414) 336-0157 for the attention of the Publishing
Records Department.

ISBN 0-8368-5650-3 (lib. bdg.)
ISBN 0-8368-5655-4 (softcover)

This North American edition first published in 2005 by
World Almanac® Library
330 West Olive Street, Suite 100
Milwaukee, WI 53212 USA

The series "The Lives of the Artists"
was created and produced by McRae Books Srl
Borgo Santa Croce, 8 – Florence (Italy)
info@mcraebooks.com
Publishers: Anne McRae and Marco Nardi

Project Editor: Loredana Agosta
Art History consultant: Roberto Carvalho de Magalhães
Text: Sean Connolly
Illustrations: Studio Stalio (Alessandro Cantucci,
Fabiano Fabbrucci, Andrea Morandi)
Graphic Design: Marco Nardi
Picture Research: Loredana Agosta
Layout: Studio Yotto
World Almanac® Library editor: JoAnn Early Macken
World Almanac® Library art direction: Tammy Gruenewald

Acknowledgments
All efforts have been made to obtain and provide compensation for the
copyright to the photos and artworks in this book in accordance with
legal provisions. Persons who may nevertheless still have claims are
requested to contact the copyright owners.
All works by Jackson Pollock: ©2005 The Estate of Jackson Pollock by SIAE, Rome.

t=top; tl=top left; tc=top center; tr=top right; c=center; cl=center left;
cr=center right; b=bottom; bl=bottom left; bc=bottom center; br=bottom
right

The publishers would like to thank the following archives who have
authorized the reproduction of the works in this book:
The Bridgeman Art Library, London/Farabola Foto, Milan: 9b, 10, 11tr, 11b,
12b, 13t, 13b, 14t, 14b, 15t, 18-19, 18tr, 21t, 21b, 22c, 24c, 26-27, 28cl, 28b, 29bl,
29c, 30, 31tr, 31b, 32cr, 33, 34bl, 38b, 39br, 43t, 44bl; ©Foto Scala, Florence:
cover, 7b, 9t, 16tl, 23t, 23b, 25t, 25b, 35t, 35b, 36b, 37t, 39cr, 41tr, 45t; ©Photo
RMN: 7cr (P.Schmidt), 16r (P.Bernard), 17, 31cl, 37b (G.Blot/ C.Jean),
40b, 41b, 42b, 43b, 44bl; Corbis/Contrasto, Milan: 16b; Photos 12,
Paris/Grazia Neri, Srl, Milan: 6b, 8bl, 18bc, 20b, 29t, 40cl, 44tr, 45br; Roger-
Voillet, Paris/ Fratelli Alinari, Florence: 42t; Marco Nardi: 7cl

The publishers would like to thank the following museums and
institutions who have authorized the reproduction of the works in this
book: Museum Folkwang, Essen: 32bl

Printed in China

1 2 3 4 5 6 7 8 9 08 07 06 05 04

cover: *Red Poppies at Argenteuil*, Musée d'Orsay, Paris
opposite: detail *Rouen Cathedral in Full Sunlight: Harmony in Blue
and Gold*, Musée d'Orsay, Paris
previous page: *Self-Portrait*, Musée d'Orsay, Paris

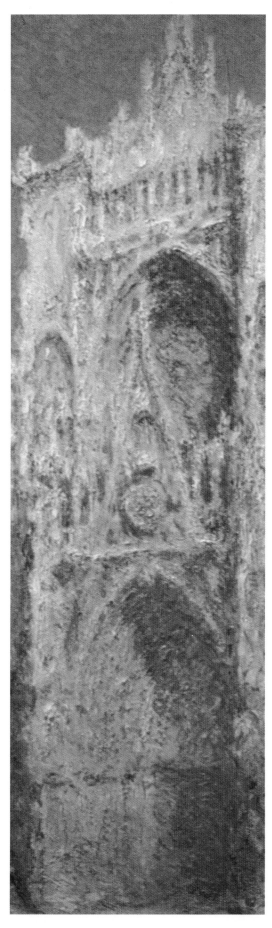

Table of Contents

Introduction

Monet's FRANCE

Le Havre · Argenteuil · Paris

Claude Monet was one of the most influential artists of the nineteenth and early twentieth centuries. He painted actively for more than sixty years, a span during which he witnessed movements that flew in the face of traditional painting techniques. Monet carved his own course, studying the world around him to capture the essence of light and color on his canvases. The work of Monet and his fellow Impressionists also paved the way for a number of later artistic approaches, which are known generally as "modern art," of which abstract art is part.

Impressionism

Monet was one of the most famous — and one of the first — of the painters who became known as the Impressionists. This group of artists, who produced their first typical works in the 1860s in France, shared a desire to capture the immediate visual impression of a subject rather than any permanent significance in what they saw. Many of the best examples of Impressionism were landscapes painted outdoors. Working in these conditions inspired the artists to examine the changing interplay of light and color. It also meant that they had to work quickly — a sudden shower or strong wind could force them to abandon a half-finished work.

▼ The Garden at Ste.-Adresse *(1867). Monet demonstrated some of the techniques that characterized much of his mature work, especially the way in which he emphasized the flattening effects of the clear light and the bright colors of the flags and flowers.*

The Wandering Eye

Claude Monet traveled widely throughout his life, usually with his painting equipment to capture what he observed. Some of his trips were forced on him by necessity, such as his London stay during the Franco-Prussian War. Other trips that were not planned as painting expeditions, such as his trip to Venice with his wife Alice, inspired him to paint just the same. At no time did Monet lose sight of his native France, and he made regular painting expeditions within his own country, often lasting for months.

▶ *Monet's trips to London (see pages 19 and 37) were artistically productive. He completed about one hundred views of London between 1899 and 1901.*

Monet in Giverny

Despite his lifelong love of travel, Monet drew great inspiration from his home in Giverny, about 25 miles (40 km) west of Paris. After initially renting the house, he was able to buy it when his career offered him more financial stability. Monet set about creating an environment that provided both a retreat and a subject. The setting inspired him in his last decades to produce his *Water Lilies* paintings. Failing eyesight served to strengthen his preoccupation with color. These works represent a culmination of many of the techniques that Monet developed when he was younger.

▶ *The Garden at Giverny (1900), painted a decade after Monet bought the property. Monet and his sons initially tended the garden. Eventually, six gardeners were needed to look after it.*

Japanese Prints

Nineteenth-century Europeans had become fascinated by Japan as an exotic and previously secret country. Japanese woodblock prints became widely available, heightening European preoccupation with the unfamiliar traditions and artistic techniques of the Japanese. Monet began collecting such prints, and he became interested in the treatment of perspective and composition, which differed greatly from the European approach dating from the Renaissance. Some of his own paintings were directly inspired by the Japanese works he had acquired.

▲ *This famous woodblock print by the Japanese artist Katsushika Hokusai (1760–1849), with its group of people arranged across the foreground, probably inspired Monet's work* The Garden at Ste.-Adresse.

▶ *This photograph shows Monet in his garden at Giverny with the Japanese footbridge in the background.*

Monet's Childhood

1840 Monet is born in Paris. He is the eldest son of a wholesale grocer, Adolphe Monet.

1845 The Monet family moves to the port city of Le Havre, at the mouth of the Seine River, where Monet's father takes over the management of the family's successful grocery and ship-provisioning business.

1848 King Louis-Philippe is overthrown in a year of Europe-wide revolutions.

1851 Louis-Napoléon Bonaparte seizes power in France. He proclaims himself Emperor Napoleon III a year later.

1855 Showing a precocious skill for drawing, Monet begins to sell caricatures around Le Havre.

Monet was born on November 14, 1840, in Paris, although the family moved to Le Havre when Monet was very young. Monet turned his early talent for drawing and observation to good effect in a series of caricatures drawn of characters in his local school as well as social "types" he observed in Le Havre.

His father had hoped that Monet would take over the family wholesale grocery business, but the boy showed little interest in commerce.

▲ *The Gare de l'Est, built between 1847 and 1850, was one of the huge train stations built in Paris to serve the expanding rail network.*

Le Havre

Monet spent his formative years in the bustling port of Le Havre, which was the main transatlantic terminus for French commercial shipping. The waterfront offered a constantly changing mix of promenading dandies, stevedores unloading foreign cargo, and ships preparing to sail to far-off destinations. The Monet family business — which included provisioning ships — no doubt heightened the young boy's interest in the sea. Seascapes and coastal scenes figured largely in his artistic output.

Paris

The mid-nineteenth century was the great age of railroad expansion, in France as well as in other countries. Paris, with its central position within the country, was an obvious hub for a rail network that fanned out to every part of France. The ease of travel to and from the capital heightened the importance of Paris as an artistic center. By the end of the nineteenth century, it was recognized as the most important cultural city in the world.

▼ *This nineteenth-century photograph of Le Havre shows the architectural variety and commercial activity near the harborfront.*

The Second Empire

After the upheaval of the French Revolution (1789–99) in the eighteenth century, followed by the empire-building and eventual defeat of Napoleon Bonaparte (1769–1821), France restored its monarchy in the early nineteenth century. In 1848, King Louis-Philippe (1773–1850) was overthrown, and a new republican government was installed. Napoleon I's nephew, Louis-Napoléon Bonaparte (1808–73) was elected president of France that same year. Within four years, however, he had abandoned his republican principles and seized outright control. In late 1852, he declared himself Emperor Napoleon III, at the heart of the Second Empire. In keeping with this imperial role, he created a fashionable court, commissioning leading artists and designers.

▲ *This contemporary portrait of Napoleon III shows him in a typical pose. He loved pageantry and uniforms.*

▶ *David's* Oath of the Horatii *(1784) exhibited some of the qualities that made his work so attractive to a self-important ruler such as Napoleon III. Its classical setting and dramatic composition helped link nineteenth-century France to the great age of the Classics.*

Art in France

Second Empire art reflected the changing tastes of France and its rulers. The works of an ardently revolutionary artist, Jacques-Louis David (1748–1825), inspired other commissions throughout the periods of Napoleon and the Monarchy and into the Second Empire. David was one of the main representatives of the neoclassical style that celebrated pageantry and heroic deeds. This approach was in perfect keeping with the grand ambitions of Napoleon III, who encouraged other artists to emulate David.

▶ *Early cameras needed long exposures to capture images, and their operators needed considerable practice to perfect their craft.*

New Advances

Artists had long been interested in ways of capturing or projecting images in a way that would help them paint with more clarity and precision. Devices such as the *camera obscura* used pinholes to allow light into a box, thereby allowing the image to be projected on the inside surface of the box. These images, however, moved in time with the original subjects. The development of photography in the 1840s brought a real advance. For the first time, still images could be captured and recorded permanently. Some artists saw photography as a useful aid; others criticized the "soulless" quality of these black-and-white images.

Monet's Caricatures

The young Monet was a skillful draftsman and could render recognizable likenesses with ease. As a teenager, he turned this skill to good use by producing a number of caricatures. Using schoolmates or characters on the Le Havre streets as his subjects, he executed dozens of works that were noted for their skill. He became confident enough to begin selling the works as a means of earning extra money. These caricatures soon became Monet's entrance into the world of fine art. The first inkling came when his aunt — herself an amateur painter — suggested that the young Monet study drawing with a local artist.

▶ *Monet's pencil-on-paper* Petit Pantheon Theatral *(People of the Theater) (1860) shows the artist's skill as a caricaturist.*

Painting Outdoors

1856 Monet meets the landscape artist Eugène Boudin, who introduces him to open-air painting.

1857 Monet's mother dies.

1858 Monet's landscape *View of Rouelles* is shown at a public exhibition in Le Havre. It is his first oil painting to be formally exhibited.

1859 Monet goes to Paris to study painting.

1860 The *Académie Suisse* in Paris is the setting for Monet's first formal artistic training.

1861 Drafted into military service, Monet enlists in a cavalry regiment and is sent to Algeria.

Monet's caricatures were sold in an art shop in Le Havre, where the landscape painter Eugène Boudin, once a part owner of the shop, first saw them. Boudin recognized Monet's talent and introduced him to open-air ("*plein air*" in French) painting. Monet was initially reluctant to paint outdoors, but he soon showed real aptitude and dedication. Despite being refused a scholarship to study in Paris, Monet decided to go anyway, persuading his father to pay. Once in Paris, he spurned the more traditional *École des Beaux-Arts* and chose instead to study at the *Académie Suisse*.

Early Works

Although the young Monet was a skilled draftsman and had an observant eye, he could not imagine himself as a painter. His contact with Eugène Boudin (1824–98), however, soon changed that. Monet's attitude changed when he saw Boudin at work, setting up outside and painting what he saw. Boudin's methods were considered unconventional because most art schools taught students to work in studios and to paint historical subjects. Monet began following Boudin's example and was soon painting scenes he observed around Le Havre.

▼ *Boudin helped get Monet's first oil painting,* View at Rouelles *(1858), hung at an exhibition in Le Havre.*

Eugène Boudin

The painter Eugène Boudin was what we might now call a maverick. He turned his back on the mainstream artistic conventions of nineteenth-century France by choosing to work outside and to paint directly from nature. For Boudin, natural light was the key to a successful landscape or seascape, and anything done from memory or from sketches back in a studio seemed artificial and false. A resident of Le Havre and the son of a sailor, Boudin was well placed to understand the changing light and colors of coastal Normandy. His works and working techniques impressed Monet and the other artists who later became Impressionists.

▲ *Boudin's* The Port at Quimper *(1857) is a good example of his ability to capture the fickle light and colors of coastal France.*

A New Paris

Emperor Napoleon III had ambitions to modernize the French capital. He called on the administrator Baron Georges-Eugène Haussmann (1809–91) to carry out his grand plans. Haussmann responded by initiating one of the largest urban renewal projects in world history. Much of medieval Paris was destroyed. In its place came new parks and squares and wide, tree-lined boulevards. These boulevards had an extra purpose: they gave mounted soldiers and police a chance to charge straight into the heart of the capital.

▲ *The Place de l'Etoile, with streets and avenues radiating out from it, was Haussmann's crowning glory.*

▶ *Haussmann was a tireless organizer who imposed his will on those around him.*

Gustave Courbet

Gustave Courbet (1819–77) was an unconventional artist who had an enormous influence on the mid-nineteenth-century French art world. Claiming to be self-taught and not troubled by preconceived notions of what was artistically acceptable, Courbet gained admiration for the realism of his paintings. His aim was not to distort or to idealize but to paint what he saw. Responding to those who favored subjects taken from classical mythology, he said: "Painting is an art of sight and should therefore concern itself with things seen."

▼ *The Painter's Studio, a Real Allegory (1855). Courbet mocked the pretension of the nineteenth-century art world and its preoccupation with history and myth.*

1860 At the *Académie Suisse,* Monet meets fellow artist Camille Pissarro, who becomes a close friend.

1862 Monet returns to France after contracting typhoid fever in Algeria. His aunt buys him out of the army. Back in Le Havre, he once more works with Boudin and the Dutch seascape painter Johan Barthold Jongkind. He returns to Paris and enters the studio of Charles Gleyre, meeting Renoir, Sisley, and Bazille.

1863 Monet and other artists regularly visit the forest at Fontainebleau and paint landscapes.

1864 Monet spends several months painting back in Normandy.

Entering the Art World

▼ Portrait of Claude Monet in Uniform *(1860) by Charles Marie Lhuillier (1825–98).*

Sent home from Algeria as an invalid, Monet returned to Le Havre in 1862. Together with his friend Boudin and the Dutch artist Johan Barthold Jongkind, he painted around Le Havre. Monet persuaded his father to subsidize a move to Paris. There he entered the studio of Charles Gleyre, where he met Pierre-Auguste Renoir, Alfred Sisley, and Jean-Frédéric Bazille. During 1863 and 1864, he periodically worked outdoors in the forest at Fontainebleau.

▶ *In a satirical caricature by Honoré Daumier (1808–79), an artist copies the work of another artist painting outdoors.*

▼ The Seine and Notre Dame in Paris *(1864), by Johan-Barthold Jongkind. The Dutch artist was another reference for the young Monet.*

In the Army
Monet had been in the middle of his artistic training at the *Académie Suisse* when he was called up for military service in 1861. He spent a year in Algeria as part of a cavalry regiment before he contracted typhoid fever. Monet was sent back to France in 1862 and was able to buy his way out of the army, a common practice in nineteenth-century Europe.

Johan Barthold Jongkind
Back home in Normandy after his stint in the army, Monet met and began working with the Dutch painter Johan Barthold Jongkind (1819–91). Jongkind had lived in France since 1846 and had acquired some fame and critical acclaim with his landscapes, especially his seascapes. Like Boudin, Jongkind worked outdoors in order to observe nature directly. Unlike Boudin, he only sketched or did quick watercolor studies outside. He then returned to the studio to complete the finished paintings in oils.

In the Painter's Studio

Monet was indebted to his family for having bought his release from military service. When he returned to study in Paris, he chose the studio of a more traditionalist painter, Charles Gleyre (1806–74). Gleyre's own work was conventional and uninspiring, but as a critic and mentor, he was tolerant and encouraging. He urged Monet and fellow students Pierre-Auguste Renoir (1841–1919), Alfred Sisley (1839–99), and Frédéric Bazille (1841–70) to follow their own impulses in order to tap the depths of their talent. The four students became good friends.

▲ The Artist's Studio *(1870), by Frédéric Bazille. Bazille's painting recalls the painters and visitors to Gleyre's studio, including (from left): Renoir, the writer Émile Zola, Monet, Édouard Manet, Bazille, and the musician Edmond Maótre.*

▼ The Road to Bas-Breau, *(Le Pavé de Chailly), (c. 1865). Monet's work during this period reflected the importance of observing nature directly, and the forest of Fontainebleau was a rich source of subject material.*

Luncheon on the Grass

▶ *A detail of* Camille Doncieux (Lady in Green) *(1866).*

By 1865, Monet was confident enough to submit his paintings to the official Salon for the first time. This was the most important showcase for artists' work, but despite the exposure, Monet slipped into financial hardship and depression. From 1868, a wealthy Le Havre patron, Louis-Joachim Gaudibert, provided Monet with a pension. This steady flow of money eased the artist's financial troubles, allowing him to concentrate more closely on his work.

A Shocking Picture

In 1863, *Le Déjeuner sur l'Herbe* (Luncheon on the Grass) by Édouard Manet (1832–83) was rejected by the Salon. The work scandalized the art establishment with its sketchy technique and use of a contemporary female nude. Manet chose to exhibit it in the Salon des Réfusés, which was a showcase of paintings rejected by the more conservative Salon (see page 22).

▲ Le Déjeuner sur l'Herbe *(1863) by Édouard Manet.*

Monet's Composition

Manet's controversial painting was done indoors in his studio. In response, in 1865–6, Monet painted his own *Déjeuner sur l'Herbe* from a study done previously outdoors with more natural and vibrant light. The work nevertheless remained unfinished.

▶ *Monet's* Study for Le Déjeuner sur l'Herbe *(1866), a full-sized painting.*

Édouard Manet

Édouard Manet came from a prosperous background that allowed him to take risks that might have been denied poorer artists. Two of his works from 1863 unsettled the Parisian art establishment: *Le Déjeuner sur l'Herbe* and *Olympia* (see page 29). In each, Manet flouted the principle that the female nude was acceptable only in a historical or mythological setting. He found himself cast as a leader of the *avant-garde* and even an inspiration for the Impressionists.

◄ *A detail of A Studio at Batignolles (1870) by Henri Fantin-Latour (1836–1904) shows Manet at work.*

▲ La Grenouillère *(1869) by Pierre-Auguste Renoir.*

Painting with Renoir

Monet had been depressed and impoverished by a series of Salon refusals in the mid-1860s. But from 1868, Monet's old Le Havre acquaintance and supporter Louis-Joachim Gaudibert began supplying him with a regular allowance. In 1869, Monet settled near Bougival on the Seine. In the nearby river resort of La Grenouillère, he was able to paint in the company of Renoir.

▼ La Grenouillère *(1869). Monet painted the same view as Renoir.*

Luncheon on the Grass

▲ Women in the Garden *(1866). The critical failure of this painting after such an investment in time and effort forced Monet to return to Normandy.*

A Refused Painting

Women in the Garden, started in summer of 1866, was the second large work Monet painted. It was an ambitious project, and its ultimate failure to garner critical acclaim contributed to Monet's depression in the late 1860s. It was painted in natural light outdoors, and at more than 8 feet (2.5 m) high, it was far larger than any other *plein-air* painting. In addition to these risks, Monet chose to depict an everyday scene from modern life — not something usually tried on such a large scale. This method was never used for a painting of these dimensions or this kind of subject matter. Not surprisingly, *Women in the Garden* was rejected by the Salon in 1867, leaving Monet downcast and considerably poorer.

▶ *Left panel of* Le Déjeuner sur l'Herbe *(1865–66). The male model is recognizably Monet's friend Bazille.*

▼ *Central panel of* Le Déjeuner sur l'Herbe *(1865–66). Monet made more than one attempt at the outdoor setting of a luncheon, repeating his intention to celebrate the informal and transitory.*

Left Unfinished

Monet's *Le Déjeuner sur l'Herbe* — unlike Manet's work of the same name — remained unfinished, although two incomplete panels as well as the completed study have survived. Monet had been trying to outdo Manet in rejecting any classical links or allusions. His models were meant to be recognizably Camille and his friends and fellow artists Bazille and Courbet. Why the work remained unfinished is still a matter of debate. Possibly Monet was unsatisfied because he could not reproduce the same vibrant light effect he had obtained in the preliminary study realized outdoors on the big canvas.

Wartime

In 1870, Monet married Camille. When the Franco-Prussian War began only months later, the couple escaped to London. There Monet came across the work of J. M. W. Turner and kept company with Camille Pissarro, who was also based in London. The two had differing approaches in their depiction of the great city: Pissarro found almost rural beauty in some of London's suburbs, while Monet tried to capture some of the essence of London's relationship with the Thames River. While in London, Monet met the adventurous and sympathetic art dealer Paul Durand-Ruel.

▶ *A statue of winged Victory erected in Berlin after the Franco-Prussian War was a symbol of Prussia's industrial and military superiority.*

The Paris Commune

Fighting in the Franco-Prussian War ended on January 28, 1871, paving the way for an eventual peace settlement that would recognize German victory. The new French government, however, soon faced a different threat — from the capital itself. Rioting on March 18, 1871, ushered in the revolutionary Paris Commune and forced the French government to flee to Versailles. After only two months — and some fierce fighting — the Commune was finally suppressed in May 1871.

The Franco-Prussian War

By 1870, France and the German state of Prussia were locked in a diplomatic dispute involving the balance of political power in Europe. Napoleon III was convinced that the German forces were badly prepared and that a quick victory would restore his own declining popularity in France. Prussian Chancellor Otto von Bismarck (1815–1898) wanted to draw in southern German states as allies and achieve victory and German unity at the same time. Bismarck's prediction was more accurate, and Napoleon III's forces were soon pinned down in eastern France. His government fell in 1870, and leaders of the Third Republic sued for peace in 1871.

▼ *Armed National Guardsmen manned barricades to protect the Paris Commune from the advancing French Army.*

Views of London

Staying in London offered Monet a respite from the tension and fighting in his own country. True to his own impulses and inspired by some of the masterpieces of the English artist J. M. W. Turner (1775–1851), Monet observed the great city in relation to its great river, the Thames. Other French artists, notably Monet's friend Pissarro, often concentrated on semirural corners of the London suburbs.

▶ Upper Norwood Crystal Palace *(1870) by Camille Pissarro (1830–1903). Pissarro was captivated by London's almost rural suburbs.*

▼ The Thames below Westminster *(1871). Monet's study of London's landmarks and the Thames River has more than an echo of Turner's earlier work.*

Argenteuil

1871 Monet's father dies. Monet returns to France, stopping in Holland on the way home. While in Holland, he paints *A Windmill at Zaandam*. The couple settles in Argenteuil, located on the Seine northwest of Paris.

1872 Friends of Monet, including Renoir, Manet, and Sisley, gravitate to Argenteuil and begin painting there, sometimes alongside each other. Monet builds a floating studio to make it easier to work on the river.

1873 Monet begins painting scenes of his home and garden, beginning a practice that becomes a lifelong inspiration.

Monet used his father's death in 1871 as as the spur to leave London and return to France. Monet and his wife Camille eventually moved to the riverside village of Argenteuil, along the Seine not far from Paris. Monet was enthralled by the interplay of color and light on the aquatic landscape and tried to capture their changing qualities in his paintings. This pleasure was evident in his eagerness to use his house, the gardens, and the surrounding countryside as the subject of many paintings. Several of Monet's painter friends were also attracted to this pleasant setting.

▼ *The Dutch countryside, with its dikes and windmills, inspired Monet to paint landscapes.*

◀ *Detail of* Meditation, or Madame Monet on the Sofa *(c. 1871). This portrait of Camille was painted while they were still in London.*

A Trip to Holland
When Monet decided to return to France, his original plan was to arrive in late May, but on the way back home, he decided to stop in Holland. Monet settled in the Amsterdam suburb of Zaandam, which offered him the chance to visit the Dutch capital (where he bought more Japanese prints) as well as to explore and paint the countryside.

The Boat Studio
Monet returned to Paris in the fall of 1871 and was appalled by the destruction and tension in the capital. In December, he and his family moved about 9 miles (15 km) down the Seine to the riverside village of Argenteuil. They lived there for seven years, during which time Monet became attached to the village and its views of the river. He even built a "floating studio," a boat that converted into a mobile workspace from which he could observe scenes that were inaccessible from the shore.

▶ The Boat Studio *(1876). Monet used his floating studio constantly during his seven years in Argenteuil.*

Other Artists in Argenteuil

Other artists — including Renoir, Sisley, and later Caillebotte, were attracted to Argenteuil, and they often painted alongside each other. These artists shared a love of painting outdoors and were as intrigued as Monet with the spectacle of natural light and the changing seasons. The works completed by these artists in the early 1870s formed the backbone of the first Impressionist exhibition (see pages 22–23) because their choice of subject matter and the manner of execution reflected their shared outlook.

Family Life in Argenteuil

Many aspects of Monet's life became settled during his years in Argenteuil. His financial troubles seemed behind him because his paintings were selling well and fetching good prices. On the domestic front, Argenteuil provided Monet and his family with their first real home. Camille and the young Jean enjoyed the relaxed, peaceful atmosphere and were models in paintings by Monet and by his friends. Some of Monet's paintings capture intimate family moments and preserve the image of young Jean as a frolicking child.

▲ Footbridge at Argenteuil *(1872) by Alfred Sisley (1839–99). The semirural charm attracted Monet and his friends.*

▼ Red Poppies at Argenteuil *(1973). Monet almost certainly used Camille (with parasol in the foreground) and young Jean as models.*

1873 Monet becomes a founding member of the Société Anonyme des Artistes, Peintres, Sculpteurs, Graveurs, Etc.

1874 The first exhibition mounted by the Société Anonyme receives a mixed critical reception. Monet's *Impression: Sunrise* inspires fierce debate.

The Impressionists

The painters who worked at Argenteuil and other like-minded French artists organized their first Paris exhibition in 1874. They stood in opposition to the conservative Salon, which opposed any sort of artistic experimentation. The exhibition created a stir and evoked some hostile responses. One critic described the group as "impressionists," implying that the works were unfinished impressions and not fully realized. Before long, the painters and supportive critics seized on this term, and the group became known as the Impressionists.

◀ *A caricature showed a pregnant woman denied entry to the Impressionist exhibition's shocking works.*

▼ The Sword Dance *(c. 1870) by Jean-Léon Gérôme (1824–1904). Gérôme was a member of the Academy and consistently argued against including "unsuitable" works in Salon exhibitions.*

The Salon

By the mid-nineteenth century, French art was dominated by the annual exhibitions held by the Salon in Paris. The Salon took its name from the Salon d'Apollon in the Louvre Museum, where the first such exhibition was held in 1667 under the auspices of the French Royal Academy of Painting and Sculpture. Being chosen for exhibition was a great honor because there were no other public exhibitions of art. The Salon used its influence to promote works that conformed to existing values in taste and decency. Artists (or works) deemed unsuitable were shunned. The virtual certainty of Salon refusal prompted Monet and others to mount the rival exhibition that ushered in the Impressionist movement.

▼ *Detail of* Portrait of Edmond Duranty *(1879) by Edgar Degas. Duranty was an influential editor and champion of the Impressionists.*

The *Société Anonyme*

Eager to mount an alternative exhibition, Monet and fifteen other artists formed the Société Anonyme des Artistes, Peintres, Sculpteurs, Graveurs, Etc. in 1873 and began recruiting other artists. "Société Anonyme" simply means "limited liability company" in French, and the company was open to anyone. Membership entitled artists to have two pictures hung, although this rule was largely ignored. All members had equal rights in electing a committee of fifteen artists. With such a commercial footing, the artists intended to exhibit independently of the Salon — and to make a profit.

The First Exhibition

The Société Anonyme held its first exhibition from April 15 to May 15, 1874 in what had been the studio of the French photographer Gaspard-Félix Nadar (1820–1910). Renoir was in charge of the committee that organized hanging the 165 works on display. Edgar Degas (1834–1917), with ten paintings, was best represented of the thirty-nine artists in the exhibition. Monet had five oil paintings and seven pastels on display. Others represented included Renoir, Pissarro, Sisley, Paul Cézanne (1839–1906), Armand Guillaumin (1841–1927), and Berthe Morisot (1841–95), the first woman to join the Impressionist movement.

Coining a Term

The art critic Louis Leroy (1821–85) was among many who scorned the works in what amounted to an alternative exhibition. His article in the satirical magazine *Le Charivari* was entitled "The Exhibition of the Impressionists." He used the term "impressionist" negatively, implying that the viewers had to guess what impression the artists had intended in their half-finished paintings. He described Monet's *Impression: Sunrise* as "wallpaper in an embryonic state."

▲ La Loge *(1874) by Pierre-Auguste Renoir was one of the few Impressionist exhibition works to escape negative criticism from the French art press.*

▼ Impression: Sunrise *(1872). The title of Monet's work inspired Leroy to call the artists represented at the exhibition "Impressionists."*

New Horizons

1876 A second Impressionist exhibition, held in the gallery of art dealer Paul Durand-Ruel, features eighteen paintings by Monet.

1877 Seven paintings of the Gare St.-Lazare are among the thirty Monet works included in the third exhibition.

1878 Camille gives birth to Michel but becomes gravely ill. Also troubled by financial worries, the family is forced to leave Argenteuil and move in with the Hoschedés.

1879 Monet contributes twenty-nine works to the fourth Impressionist exhibition in April. Camille dies in September.

Monet and other Impressionists shrugged off any hostile critical reaction. Monet's works began to show a vibrant quality in their use of color. In his efforts to capture the fleeting effects of light and color, Monet painted quickly and loaded his short brushstrokes with individual colors. Even paintings of urban scenes and the darkest winter days revealed an astonishing range of colors in Monet's works of this period.

◀ *Japanese prints with their exotic embellishments captivated the French art world in the early 1870s. Critics and painters sought to celebrate Japanese art.*

▶ *Detail of* Arrangement in Flesh Color and Black: Portrait of Théodore Duret *(1883–4) by James Whistler (1834–1903).*

Japanese Art

Despite his inclination toward experiment and his association with successive Impressionist exhibitions, Monet kept in touch with popular taste. During the 1870s, Japanese prints, which had already inspired the artist, enjoyed enormous popularity in Paris. Monet saw a way of combining his own love of Japanese art with current popular demand — and also the chance for lucrative sales. He included a portrait of his wife Camille in Japanese costume in the second Impressionist exhibition of 1876.

Théodore Duret

Monet and other Impressionists depended on the support (and sometimes buying power) of influential people who could generate good publicity. One of the most important was the writer and art collector Théodore Duret (1838–1927), who had already written favorably about the Impressionists in his book, *Les Peintures Françaises en 1867* (French Painters of 1867). His writing helped build the reputation of the Impressionists within the wider art world. Duret remained an ardent patron, forging intimate relationships with the Impressionists and other controversial artists such as James Whistler (1834–1903).

◀ La Japonaise (Camille Monet in Japanese Costume) *(1876). Monet combined a number of features to impress an audience fascinated with Japanese art.*

Celebration and Pain

Paris staged a Universal Exhibition in 1878, and Monet took the opportunity to paint street scenes of the festivities. That same year, Camille gave birth to the couple's second son, Michel, but she did not recover from the birth. She died in September 1879, leaving Monet grief stricken. He was also in a difficult financial position and had to move in with wealthy friends, the Hoschedés.

The Railroad

The vast fairs, called universal expositions, that were so popular in nineteenth-century Europe came in response to the technological progress triggered by the Industrial Revolution. Nowhere was this progress as advanced — or as celebrated — as with the railroads. Far-reaching rail networks crisscrossed France and other industrialized countries. Serving as hubs for these networks were huge train stations in major cities. Monet was fascinated by Gare Saint-Lazare, the massive Parisian station that was the terminus of the line running in from Argenteuil. In 1877, he began work on twelve paintings of the station, capturing its cathedral-like spaces and the frantic people rushing around within it.

▼ *Trains enabled people to travel around France with an ease that seemed unimaginable fifty years earlier.*

▲ The Rue Montorgueil, 30th of June 1878 *(1878). Monet's work was beginning to focus more and more on color.*

▼ The Gare St.-Lazare *(1877). Monet was fascinated by the interplay of smoke and steam in the light filtering down from the enormous glass roof.*

Developing a Vision

By the early 1880s, the Impressionists began to unravel as a cohesive group, although individual members occasionally worked together. Monet did not take part in the fifth or sixth Impressionist shows, but he exhibited again in the seventh with the fruits of his painting trips outside of Paris. In 1883, Monet moved his family to a rented house in Giverny (which, like Argenteuil, was also on the Seine), where he was based for the rest of his life.

1880 Monet does not participate in the fifth Impressionist exhibition. He upsets some other Impressionists by exhibiting a painting in the Salon that same year.

1881 Once more, Monet does not exhibit with the Impressionists (in their sixth group show). He begins making painting trips to the Channel coast. In December, he sets up home with Alice Hoschedé and their eight children at Poissy.

1882 Monet takes part in the seventh Impressionist exhibition with thirty-five works.

1883 Art dealer Paul Durand-Ruel organizes a Monet show with fifty-six paintings. In April, Monet moves the extended family to Giverny.

Monet's Dealer

Monet's friendship with the art dealer Paul Durand-Ruel (1831–1922) dated back to his stay in London during 1870 and 1871 (see pages 18–19). Durand-Ruel had remained a champion of Monet and later of the other Impressionists. In addition to his welcome support and friendship, Durand-Ruel bought Monet's works at good prices and helped secure other sales. In 1883, he even staged a one-man show of Monet's works. Initially a lone voice in support of the Impressionists, Durand-Ruel occasionally came close to bankruptcy because of his generosity.

▼ *Paul Durand-Ruel's correspondence with Monet shows the support he provided.*

Edgar Degas

The artist who exhibited the most works in the first Impressionist show was the painter and sculptor Edgar Degas. In spite of his active participation, however, he differed from most other Impressionists. Like Édouard Manet, he came from a comfortable background and was less concerned with financial pressure. Like Manet, he also had sound academic training. Degas worked to achieve some of the same effects as the Impressionists — that of capturing the fleeting or ephemeral — but he never completed his works outdoors. Instead, he returned to his studio with sketches to be refined into oil paintings or sculptures. Degas's increasing influence over the exhibitions, coupled with his championing of realism, led to rifts with Monet and other Impressionists.

◀ Little Dancer *(1880), sculpture by Edgar Degas. To capture the texture, Degas combined bronze with real fabric.*

▶ Cliff at Dieppe *(1882). Monet began taking extended painting trips to the northern French coast in a productive burst of activity in the early 1880s.*

A New Love

When Ernest Hoschedé, Monet's friend and patron, was declared bankrupt in 1878, his wife Alice and their six children moved in with the Monets and their two sons. Alice helped nurse Camille during the last stages of her illness following the traumatic birth of Michel. After Camille's death in 1879, Alice and Monet began a relationship of their own. Ernest was now living alone in Paris but maintaining ties with the Impressionists. In 1881, Monet, Alice, and their eight children set up house in Poissy. Two years later, they moved to a rented house in Giverny, which was an inspiration for the rest of Monet's working life.

▶ *Alice Hoschedé, who became Monet's second wife in 1892 following Ernest Hoschedé's death.*

Gaining Recognition

1883 Monet begins painting his first river scenes around Giverny.

1884 Monet spends several months painting the Mediterranean coast in Italy and France.

1885 Georges Petit's fourth *Exposition Internationale* includes works by Monet.

1886 Monet spends several months painting on the Normandy coast.

1888 Monet spends four months painting on the Mediterranean coast. He sells ten paintings to Vincent van Gogh's brother Theo.

1889 Monet spends the spring painting in the Creuse Valley. His paintings and Rodin's sculptures feature in a major exhibition staged by Petit.

By the mid-1880s, Monet's paintings were selling well and commanding high prices. Durand-Ruel continued to champion his work and that of other Impressionists. Following the one-man show of Monet's work in 1883, he organized the first extensive Impressionist exhibition in the United States in 1886. In 1889, Monet exhibited with France's most celebrated sculptor, Auguste Rodin. He parted company with many of the other Impressionists at this time, largely in response to the new "scientific" approach being used by Seurat and Signac.

▲ *A poster for Zola's play,* L'Assommoir *(The Drunkard), based on his bestselling 1877 novel.*

Monet and the Literary World

Monet and other Impressionists became acquainted with writers and poets, sounding each other out for inspiration. In 1884, Durand-Ruel introduced Monet to the author Octave Mirbeau (1850–1917), who supported Monet's works in his articles in *La France*. Through Berthe Morisot, another of the Impressionists, Monet and Renoir met the poet Stéphane Mallarmé (1842–98). The relationship of the writer Èmile Zola (1840–1902) — France's bestselling author in the 1880s — and the Impressionists was more troubled. A childhood friend of Cézanne and later a defender of Manet, Zola published *L'Œuvre* (The Masterpiece) in 1886, offending several Impressionists in the process. Monet and Cézanne both felt that the tragic hero (an artist like the Impressionists) had been based on them.

▲ Bathers at Asnières *(1884) by Georges Seurat (1859–91). Seen from a distance, the tiny dots of pure color melt to compose the image and a sense of atmosphere.*

A New Approach

In the mid-1880s, Georges Seurat (1859–91) and Paul Signac (1863–1935) pioneered a new artistic approach — Pointillism — that was as revolutionary as Impressionism had seemed a decade earlier. Following scientific analysis of light and color, they applied dots of pure color to achieve an intended shade, composing images with an eye to geometry and harmony. The critic Félix Fénéon (1861–1944) approved of this scientific approach to painting and called it neo-impressionism.

◀ Portrait of Stéphane Mallarmé *(1892) by Pierre-Auguste Renoir. Mallarmé had praised the Impressionists from the time of their first exhibition.*

Love for the Sea

Despite Monet's growing success in the Paris art world — and the inspiration and support he drew from critics, patrons, and artists — he remained true to his original preference for painting outdoors. In these years, he undertook frequent and prolonged trips to the French coast. There he set up his equipment and painted the changing coastal scenes. In 1886, he had a particularly productive stay on the island of Belle-Île in Brittany, where he painted the effects of the violent weather.

▲ Storm off the Belle-Île Coast *(1886). Monet's short and rapid brushstrokes perfectly convey the sense of movement.*

Monet and Rodin

The sculptor Auguste Rodin (1840–1917) was born in the same year as Monet, and by the late 1880s, the two artists had reached the summits of their respective media. During the summer of 1889, the art dealer Georges Petit (1856–1920) organized a retrospective exhibition of the works of the two artists. Monet alone had about 150 of his paintings exhibited. The show was an enormous success, with critics especially impressed with a series of fourteen works that Monet had painted of the same scene in the Massif Central region of France.

◄ The Burghers of Calais *(1884–6), by Auguste Rodin. The sculptor's exploration of painful emotion unsettled the Calais officials who had commissioned the work.*

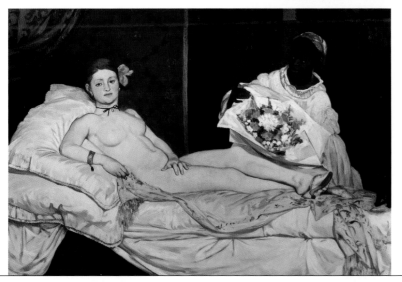

A Valuable Work of Art

Édouard Manet died in 1883, leaving his widow in difficult financial circumstances. Monet decided to help her by raising 20,000 francs to buy Manet's *Olympia* for the state. In doing so, Monet raised the profile of Manet and other avant-garde artists. Monet spent a year organizing this deal, and in 1890, he received a guarantee that the French government would receive the work and eventually hang it in the Louvre Museum.

◄ Olympia *(1863) by Édouard Manet. Monet's plan for its display incensed conservatives who were shocked by the blatant nudity and unconventional use of light and dark.*

Settling Down

▼ The Haystacks, *or* The End of the Summer, Morning *(1891). Monet captured the bittersweet qualities of the late summer sun.*

In 1890, Monet was able to buy the Giverny house he had rented for years. He began to create the shimmering water garden that inspired many of his later paintings. On the artistic front, he completed many paintings of haystacks and poplars. Many of these returned to an identical point of view, capturing the same scene in a different light or at a different time of year.

Experiments with Light and Color

Aware that the appearance of things changes with the conditions in which they are observed, Monet decided to single out a particular scene, captured from a certain vantage point, and to paint it many times in different conditions of light and weather. He began his experiments with series paintings with a number of works concentrating on haystacks in the fields near his house in Giverny. He worked on several paintings at once, changing from one canvas to another as the day's light and colors changed.

Monet's Haystacks

With his eyes attuned to the slightest difference in light or color, Monet would stand in a farmer's field, waiting to capture and record a fleeting impression on one of his canvases. The writer Guy de Maupassant (1850–93), visiting Giverny, described the impression that the artist himself made: "Actually, he was no longer a painter, but a hunter." Monet was seeking to record not just the immediate instant but a series of instants throughout the year. As winter approached, he even paid the farmer to keep his haystacks in place, so many of the most memorable paintings are snow scenes.

Images of Rural Life

In choosing haystacks as his subject, Monet continued an established tradition in French art. Before Monet, though, artists had chosen to depict haystacks not as the focus of the paintings but as symbols of rural prosperity. In Monet's works, they became "characters" in their own right, reacting to the changing effects of nightfall, brooding clouds, or morning sunshine. In this way, Monet turned the tradition on its head and brought it in line with Impressionist aims.

◄ *Monet's pink stucco house, Le Pressoir, was one of the largest buildings in Giverny, but that was not surprising in a village numbering fewer than three hundred inhabitants. Monet's first act on buying the property was to convert the large kitchen garden into a garden of his own design.*

▲ Haystacks: Autumn *(1868–74) by Jean-François Millet. In this landscape, the haystacks are the central feature, but they are linked to Millet's ideas about rural life in general.*

Settling Down in Giverny

Le Pressoir, Monet's house in Giverny, had already provided the artist with a secure base to return to after his painting expeditions and dealings with the Paris art world. It took on a new importance after he became its owner in 1890. He and Alice had an ideal domestic environment in which to raise their children. Just as important, the property became a subject in its own right, inspiring Monet for more than three more decades.

Poplars

The poplars growing along the banks of the nearby Epte River became the subject for Monet's second exercise in series painting. As with the haystacks, he studied particular scenes and worked on several canvases at once. In all, he completed twenty-four poplar paintings, all but four done in his floating studio (see page 20). Special grooves on the floor of the boat allowed a number of canvases to be supported at the same time.

► The Three Poplar Trees, Autumn *(1891). The success of the haystack paintings inspired Monet to continue his exploration of light and color.*

Series Paintings

1892 Monet spends February to April painting Rouen Cathedral, beginning work weeks before his poplar paintings are exhibited at Durand-Ruel's gallery. In July, he marries Alice Hoschedé just days before his stepdaughter Suzanne marries the American painter Theodore Butler (1861–1936).

1893 Once more, Monet spends February–April painting Rouen Cathedral. In the summer, he begins the construction of the water garden at Giverny.

1894 The painters Paul Cézanne and Mary Cassatt (1844–1926) visit Monet in Giverny.

Monet's haystack paintings were enormously successful, both critically and in commercial terms. Their success gave Monet the confidence to embark on a far more ambitious and time-consuming project even before his poplar paintings had been sent off to Durand-Ruel. From 1892 through 1894, Monet occupied himself with a new task: painting a series of studies of the façade of Rouen Cathedral, once more seen in a variety of light and weather conditions.

Rouen Cathedral

The works concentrating on Rouen Cathedral were to become perhaps Monet's most significant series paintings. He had mastered his approach with his haystack and poplar paintings in previous years and was prepared — and financially solvent enough — to devote several years to this project. He rented a room in a store opposite the Cathedral, although he had to move to a window next door, creating two viewpoints in the series. Despite several lengthy interruptions, Monet worked from 1892 to 1894 and exhibited the thirty pictures the following year.

◄ Rouen Cathedral: the Portal, Morning Fog *(1893). Monet's vantage point was across the square from the Cathedral.*

▲ Rouen Cathedral in the Setting Sun *(1892–4). The western façade allowed Monet to concentrate on direct afternoon and evening light.*

▲ Rouen Cathedral in Full Sunlight: Harmony in Blue and Gold *(1894). The later works became studies in color and light, concentrating even less on the detail of the Cathedral façade.*

1895 Monet spends three months visiting Norway and completing a number of works. Back in Giverny for the summer, he begins building the Japanese bridge.

1896–7 Monet divides his painting time between the Normandy coast (winter and spring) and the banks of the Seine.

1897 Monet's son Jean marries Blanche Hoschedé.

1898 A successful exhibition at Petit's gallery includes series paintings of the Normandy coast and *Early Morning on the Seine.*

1899 Monet begins the first series of paintings of his Giverny water garden and footbridge.

Testing His Ideas

Throughout the late 1890s, Monet continued his habit of taking extended painting trips within France. An especially fruitful pair of locations (coastal Normandy and the banks of the Seine) inspired yet more brilliant series paintings. He also had a lengthy visit to Norway, where he was able to study the wintry conditions and mountainous landscape for yet more paintings. At the same time, the water garden and footbridge at Giverny were becoming touchstones for his art. He began his first Giverny series paintings in 1899.

▲ *A poster advertising the first comedy film ever,* The Waterer Watered, *produced by the Lumière brothers.*

The Moving Image

On December 28, 1895, the brothers Auguste (1862–1954) and Louis (1864–1948) Lumière (their surname, appropriately, means "light" in French) staged the world's first public screening of motion pictures. The ten films lasted no more than twenty minutes in total, but the effect was astounding. People screamed and even fled the Parisian café that served as the groundbreaking movie theater. Scenes of trains approaching the screen were terrifying for an audience that was familiar only with still images or the most basic moving displays. Unaware that they had, in fact, created an art form, the brothers considered themselves lucky to have made a profit with a medium that they felt would soon be considered a passing fad.

▼ Mount Kolsaas in Norway *(1895). Monet likened the mountain to Mount Fuji, which was familiar to him from Japanese prints.*

Monet in Norway

Having finished his Rouen Cathedral series, Monet visited his stepson Jacques Hoschedé in Norway. What began as a family visit to Christiania (present-day Oslo) developed into a painting expedition when Jacques took him to the village of Sandviken. Monet was enthralled by the spectacular winter scenery. Working through the winter of 1894–5, he completed a series of paintings. Many of them were of Mount Kolsaas.

The Japanese Bridge

In 1893, Monet purchased several acres of land across the tracks from his house in Giverny. He excavated and enlarged an existing pond, diverting a little river to feed the pond. There he put water lilies imported from Japan, and around it he planted dozens of trees and flowering shrubs. Monet also oversaw designs for a footbridge that was built over the pond. It was soon dubbed the "Japanese Footbridge," in part because a screen of bamboo grew behind it. In 1895, he began painting the bridge, and the works from 1899 were exhibited in Durand-Ruel's gallery.

▼ Branch of the Seine near Giverny *(1897).* *In keeping with the subject, Monet emphasized the limpid and translucent qualities of the paint.*

◄ *Monet's 1898 exhibition at Georges Petit's gallery featured paintings from the Normandy coast as well as the* Early Morning on the Seine *series. The newspaper* Le Gaulois *even devoted a special supplement to the exhibition.*

▲ White Water Lilies *(1899). The footbridge featured in manyof Monet's paintings of his gardens, often forming a harmonious visual "punctuation."*

Painting at Dawn

Monet's love of light led him to complete a series of paintings that became known as *Early Morning on the Seine.* In 1896 and 1897, he returned to Giverny from the Normandy coast. In the warmer months, he got up before dawn to capture the beautiful light and the fog along the riverside at sunrise. Seventeen of these works drew critical acclaim at a one-man show in Georges Petit's gallery in 1898.

New Freedoms

1900 Monet spends several months painting in London, continuing work begun in 1899. An exhibition at Durand-Ruel's gallery includes the first water garden series.

1901 After the third and final painting trip to London, Monet returns to Giverny. He enlarges the water garden and buys an automobile.

1903 Paul Gauguin dies.

1904 The London paintings are exhibited with Durand-Ruel in May. In October, Monet and his wife drive to Spain to see the work of Velázquez.

With the turn of the new century, Monet enjoyed a preeminent position in the world of French painting. He returned to paint London in the series fashion he found so inspiring thirty years before. In 1903, Monet began another series dedicated to his water lily pond at Giverny, which by this time had reached maturity and was overhung with willows and bamboo fronds.

▶ *A Citroën 5CV of 1900, similar to the model of automobile Monet bought in 1901. The invention of the automobile revolutionized travel as much as trains had fifty years earlier.*

▶ *A late nineteenth-century vase featuring the sweeping floral motifs that blossomed in France.*

Monet on the Go

Monet's wealth allowed him to afford one of the symbols of early twentieth-century progress — the automobile. Monet relished the thrill of being driven at high speed through the countryside. He left the driving to a chauffeur who also worked as mechanic, studio assistant, and wine steward. In 1904, Monet and his wife Alice drove to Madrid to see the works of Diego Velázquez (1599–1660) in the Prado Museum. Monet later drove to Italy (1908) and Switzerland (1915).

▼ Two Women on the Beach *(1891) by Paul Gauguin, who was inspired by Polynesian culture.*

Decorative Arts

French decorative arts had been stifled by the academic tradition just as painting had before the Impressionist breakthrough. By the late 1890s, however, the French could look at Britain's thriving arts and crafts movement in their search to develop their own style. Open to Japanese and other "exotic" influences, they used floral designs to underpin a style that became known as *Art Nouveau* (meaning "new art" in French).

Paul Gauguin

One of the most important artists to challenge the supremacy of Impressionism was Paul Gauguin (1848–1903). He was initially attracted to the aims and techniques of the Impressionists, and his works were included in the Impressionist exhibitions of 1879 and 1886. From then on, however, he began to reject the fragmented color and ephemeral qualities of Impressionism in favor of a style that laid large, flat areas of color on the canvas and then surrounded them with thick outlines. His "synthesis" style was a break with tradition, eventually inspiring the Fauves ("wild beasts") and Expressionist painters. From the 1890s, Gauguin became fascinated with the art and traditions of the Polynesian islands. He visited Tahiti and eventually settled in the Marquesas Islands.

Return to London

In late 1899, and for part of the next two years, Monet spent months in London working on a series of paintings. He had been to London three decades earlier when he painted the newly completed Houses of Parliament (see pages 18–19). His later series showed the same buildings as indistinct silhouettes looming by the Thames River. The series actually concentrates on light and water in relation to the Thames or through a curtain of fog. Monet worked on several canvases at once, flitting from one to another in response to the changing conditions. The whole process was exhausting, and when he returned to Giverny, not a single painting was finished. Casting aside initial disappointment, he eventually finished thirty-seven paintings, which were exhibited in 1904.

▼ Nymphéas *(1908). Of his water lily series (Nymphéas is the botanical name for one type), Monet wrote: "These landscapes of water and reflection have become my obsession."*

▲ The Houses of Parliament in London *(1900). Monet captured the changing and translucent qualities of London in a way that recalled the masterpieces of Turner.*

▲ *Returning to London as a prosperous artist, Monet could afford to stay at the newly built and decidedly luxurious Savoy Hotel.*

Reflections in the Water

Even while he worked to complete the London series, Monet began painting his Giverny gardens, especially the pond. Wild rumors, based on the public's fascination with Monet's methods, suggested that he had 150 canvases in process. The real figure is more like eighty — still a great number. As with the London paintings, Monet was fascinated with water. In these Giverny paintings, he concentrated on the surface of the water, often capturing fleeting images of clouds and foliage reflected on the surface of the pond.

1908 Monet and Alice visit Venice. He spends two months painting there.

1909 An exhibition at Durand-Ruel's gallery features forty-eight of the water lily series.

1911 Monet's wife Alice dies in May. Monet returns to work in the autumn.

1912 The Venice paintings are exhibited at the Bernheim-Jeune Gallery. Monet has cataracts diagnosed in both eyes.

1913 Monet travels to Switzerland.

1914 World War I begins. Monet's son Jean dies, and his widow, Blanche, moves into Monet's house.

▼ Venice. The Doge Palace *(c. 1908). Monet was fascinated by the interplay of water and architecture in Venice.*

Learning to See Again

▼ *Pince-nez glasses were popular, but Monet (like fellow myopic Paul Cézanne) refused to wear any sort of eyeglasses for years.*

By his mid-sixties, Monet was still painting and traveling actively, but his health began to deteriorate. In particular, he suffered from cataracts. Monet's blurred vision paradoxically matched the direction in which his art had been traveling, with its preference for color over distinct delineation of every object. The eyesight problems also helped — or forced — Monet to look harder at what he saw. He produced some magical evocations of light, color, and water, both at home and in Venice.

CLAUDE MONET

"Venise"

Neuf reproductions de Tableaux
(un fac-similé et huit phototypies)

Avec une Préface
par
OCTAVE MIRBEAU

BERNHEIM-JEUNE & Cⁱᵉ
Experts près la Cour d'Appel
15, Rue Richepanse
25, Boulevard de la Madeleine
36, Avenue de l'Opéra
PARIS

▲ *An illustrated album commemorated the 1912 exhibition of Monet's paintings of Venice.*

A Trip to Venice

Monet and Alice Monet traveled to Venice at the end of 1908. It was their last trip together before Alice's death in 1911. Monet wanted to rest, but once in Venice, he could not prevent himself from picking up a paintbrush. He returned to Giverny with nearly forty canvases, but they were in an even more unfinished state than his London works seven years earlier. Monet had simply roughed in the canvases while in Venice. Completing them in France, far way from the actual sites, proved difficult. When Monet agreed to exhibit twenty-nine of them in 1912, he considered them souvenirs of his trip rather than full-scale artistic works like other paintings of the same period.

▶ *Grand Canal, Venice (1908). The domed church of Santa Maria della Salute is a shadowy presence like the depictions of the Houses of Parliament in Monet's London series.*

Monet's Vision

Monet had long suffered from a degree of myopia (nearsightedness), although he did not see it as a huge problem. Once, having tried on a pair of eyeglasses, Monet exclaimed: "My God, I'm seeing just like Bouguereau." (The clearly delineated paintings by William-Adolphe Bouguereau (1825–1905) had been mocked by the Impressionists.) By 1908, however, it became clear that Monet was suffering from cataracts, which threatened his sight in both eyes. He resisted having corrective surgery for years, but the condition worsened, darkening the hues he perceived and painted. In 1922, Monet agreed to a series of cataract operations. These succeeded, although Monet complained that he could no longer distinguish certain colors after the operations. Luckily, corrective glasses enabled him to work through his last years.

◀ Unique Forms of Continuity in Space *(1913) by Umberto Boccioni (1882–1916).*

Art in Italy: Futurism

Only two years after Monet's visit, Venice saw a one-man exhibition that sent shock waves through the art world. The works were by Umberto Boccioni (1882–1916), a leading member of the Futurist movement. The movement was born a year earlier when the Italian poet Filippo Tomasso Marinetti (1876–1944) published the *Futurist Manifesto* in the French newspaper *Le Figaro*. In this and subsequent manifestos, the Futurists saw their work as a response to a decaying cultural void in an age of speed and mechanization. Their art was a celebration of speed, machinery, and even violence, all of which would free Western art from the weight of the past.

Water Lilies

Monet's huge studio at Giverny enabled him to work on paintings much larger than any he had completed before. In his last decade, he began work on twelve large canvases of water lilies, the *Grandes Décorations*, which he had promised to give to the state as a response to the Armistice of 1918. With few examples of eighty-year-old artists taking on huge new projects, Monet struggled against fatigue, his delicate eyesight, and lung cancer to create works that are startling in their modernity. Almost devoid of real subject matter, these paintings succeed with their marvelous use of color. Monet was still painting when he died on December 5, 1926.

A New Studio

Monet's new studio was especially created to accommodate the huge works he was creating in his last years. Measuring 75 feet (23 m) long by 40 feet (12 m) wide and with a ceiling reaching 50 feet (15) high, it gave the artist ample space. Trusses from the walls provided all the strength, so no vertical supports marred the internal space. Skylights allowed natural light to flood down into the studio, making it an ideal working environment.

◄ *Monet spent all the daylight hours at work, only receiving visitors when the last light left the studio.*

Monet's Self-Portraits

Monet painted very few self-portraits, but late in his career, he was persuaded to undertake some more of these works. It took a very special and influential friend, Georges Clemenceau (1841–1929), to convince Monet to interrupt his obsession with Giverny scenes. Clemenceau, who became prime minister of France in 1917, had known Monet since the 1860s. In 1900, he bought a country house near Giverny and became a frequent visitor. The intimacy deepened after the death of Monet's wife Alice and his eldest son Jean. Clemenceau was privy to Monet's private plans, and he was an ardent supporter of his friend's talent. Despite Clemenceau's urgings, Monet did not consider the self-portraits to be great successes and stopped painting them.

▶ Self-Portrait *(1917). Monet played off splashes of color to execute the portrait. He gave it to Clemenceau, who in turn donated it to the Louvre Museum the year after Monet died.*

The End of World War I

The protracted fighting of World War I (1914–18) saw millions die in a series of battles that sometimes gained or lost only a few yards. Georges Clemenceau's predictions about the German arms buildup before the war had been ignored, but he soon proved right. Clemenceau was called to form a government in 1917 when French morale was very low. He restored his nation's fighting spirit in keeping with his nickname ("the Tiger") and helped ensure Germany's defeat in 1918. Clemenceau presided over the Paris Peace Conference in 1919, ensuring that France regained land lost in 1871.

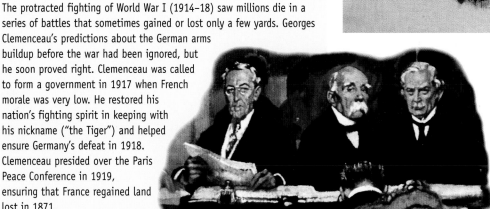

◀ *Allied leaders at the Paris Peace Conference: from left, U.S. President Woodrow Wilson, French Premier Clemenceau, and British Prime Minister David Lloyd George.*

▼ *The left and central panels of the triptych* The Clouds *(1922–6). Monet began work on these the year he left the water lily paintings to the state.*

◀ *A photograph of Monet's Water Lilies in the oval gallery of the Musée de l'Orangerie, taken around the time of its opening in 1927.*

▼ *A plan of the reconfigured rooms in the Orangerie showing the arrangement of Monet's twenty-two panels. According to the agreement, no other paintings or sculpture could ever be displayed in the rooms, and the paintings could not be varnished.*

A Museum for Monet's Works

Monet's proposed gift of his *Grandes Décorations* led to a number of problems. Their huge scale meant that an expensive new building would need to be constructed in Paris to house as-yet unfinished works by an aging artist. Monet viewed any debate on the subject as a personal rebuff. Eventually, Monet's dear friend Clemenceau used his influence to work out a compromise. Rather than housing the works in a circular room (Monet's initial preference), the long and narrow Orangerie of the Tuilerie Gardens was reconfigured into two elliptical rooms. Monet's twenty-two panels were installed there in 1927, a year after his death.

The Clouds	Morning with Willows
The Setting Sun	Green Reflections	Reflections of Trees	The Two Willows
Morning	Clear Morning with Willows

▼ *The central and right panels of the triptych* Clear Morning with Willows *(1922–6). Monet saw his monumental panels as a cyclorama with paintings surrounding the viewer in the gallery.*

▲ The House Seen from the Rose Garden *(1922). The warm — very nearly hot — hues of the foliage, achieved through thick application of color, were a far cry from the diffuse treatment of similar scenes in Monet's earlier paintings.*

Paris, Capital of Art and Culture

In the 1920s and 1930s, Paris was the world capital of art, music, fashion, and literature. It attracted foreign talents as varied as James Joyce (1882–1941), Ernest Hemingway (1899–1961), Pablo Picasso (1881–1973), and Amedeo Modigliani (1884–1920). At the same time, Paris nurtured the achievements not only of Monet, but of other French artists such as Henri Matisse (1869–1954) and Georges Braque (1882–1963). New movements, such as Dadaism and surrealism, blossomed in this atmosphere. Paris also hosted a number of important cultural exhibitions, including the 1925 international Art Deco exhibition, which showcased the works of a new generation of decorative artists.

Last Works

Monet's last works, which together would comprise the monumental *Grandes Décorations*, were remarkable for their technique and approach to color. Monet, defying his age to work with feverish intensity, loaded his brush with color and applied paint boldly on the canvas. Splashes of color seemed to vie for attention or even clash in some parts of the huge works. This boldness was at least partly the result of Monet's eyesight — his color perception in particular. The cataract operations (see page 39) had been successful, but even with corrective glasses, he saw first a yellowish color, then a blue, in everything around him. The confidence with which Monet "painted through" these problems made these late paintings as revolutionary and modern as those of the Fauves and Expressionists.

▶ *A poster advertises the* Exposition Internationale des Arts Décoratifs, *the movement that would soon be known by the shortened form Art Deco.*

Monet's Legacy

1927 The rooms housing Monet's *Grandes Décorations* in the Musée de l'Orangerie open to the public.

1947 The Jeu de Paume in the Tuileries Gardens, Paris, becomes the Musée de l'Impressionnisme, and all the Impressionist paintings from the Louvre are moved there.

1940s–50s Action painting, an abstract style best represented by the American artist Jackson Pollock, recalls the techniques of Monet in his last works.

1960 New York's Museum of Modern Art stages a Monet retrospective, which helps redress a decline in his reputation.

1966 On the death of Monet's son Michel, the house and gardens at Giverny are left to the Académie des Beaux-Arts.

1978 Monet's *The Railroad Bridge at Argenteuil* (1873) sells in London for more than $1 million (six times more than it fetched in 1963).

Monet is rightly remembered as the leading light in the Impressionist movement as well as for his longevity and remarkable ability to develop his ideas even while fighting blindness in his eighties. His increasingly bold use of brushwork, coupled with his growing preoccupation with color, showed that he had already moved far beyond simple representation by the time of his last works.

▼ *A photograph of Monet in his eighties holding his palette. His devotion to observation and painting was undiminished even in the days just before his death.*

The Last of the Impressionists

Monet outlived his contemporaries in the Impressionist movement but still found the energy and inspiration to create. This almost superhuman effort of a man in his eighties alone would have ensured the lasting reputation of Monet, but his legacy was built on more than mere longevity. In his last years, Monet showed that he never lost the drive to explore new means of observing and representing the world. He is remembered not only as one of the most famous Impressionists but as an artist who freed others to continue his explorations.

▼ *Detail of* Venice. The Doge Palace *(see page 38) shows Monet's open brushwork and distinctive use of color. His signature is on the right.*

Monet, a Modern Artist

Despite being so closely linked to Impressionism, Monet remained an independent experimenter whose work many art historians consider to be the foundation for modern art. Even some of Monet's Impressionist works of the 1870s began to show a self-conscious awareness of their existence as paintings with their celebration of color and scant regard for delineation. The later series paintings showed that subject matter was less important than the paintings themselves. By the end of Monet's life, the painter was really ushering in the age of the abstract with his huge paintings — ostensibly of water lilies but in reality celebrations of light and color.

▲ Number 1 *(1948) by Jackson Pollock. Action painting worked to release the inner value of the painting itself, not to match a viewer's expectations.*

Jackson Pollock

One modern artist whose work recalls that of Monet was Jackson Pollock (1912–56). Pollock was an abstract artist who suddenly, in 1947, developed the style of action painting that is sometimes called "drip and splash." He would drip, pour, or even fling paint down onto a canvas on the floor. Inspired by Monet's thickly laden brush strokes, he worked the paint into the canvas with sticks or knives.

◀ *Jackson Pollock at work applying dripping paint onto the canvas.*

▼ *Monet's beloved pond as it appears today. Giverny's immense popularity is due in part to its proximity to Paris.*

Giverny Today

When Monet's son Michel died in 1966, the house and gardens at Giverny were bequeathed to the Académie des Beaux-Arts. They now comprise a major museum and important cultural landmark for art lovers eager to learn more about Monet and the Impressionists. Many visitors combine a visit to Giverny with stops at other places in the Seine Basin that inspired Monet and the Impressionists. Argenteuil, Bougival, Poissy, and Vétheuil are linked — as they were in Monet's day — by the Seine train line running from Paris.

Glossary

abstract A style of art that does not represent objects as they appear in reality but reduces and simplifies forms and objects. Abstract art abandons the traditional principle that art must imitate nature.

Art Deco A style of design and interior decoration, popular in the 1920s and 1930s, that uses stylized, geometric shapes to create objects of fine workmanship. It got its name from the 1925 *Exposition Internationale des Arts Décoratifs et Industriels Modernes* held in Paris.

Art Nouveau An ornamental style of European and U.S. art that lasted from 1890 to 1910, characterized by the use of long, curving lines based on plant forms. This so-called "new" style (the word nouveau means "new" in French) was applied primarily to architecture, interior design, jewelry, glass design, and illustration.

bankruptcy Complete inability to pay one's debts.

cataract A growth on the eye that clouds the lens and prevents light from entering, causing a slow loss of sight.

caricature An amusing portrait or representation of a person in which certain features are intentionally exaggerated.

classical Term used to describe works of art from ancient Greece or Rome, or works that have the same characteristics as the works of ancient Greece or Rome.

composition The arrangement of the parts of something. Term used to refer to the way in which objects are arranged, usually in a painting or sculpture.

cyclorama A large pictorial representation or group of paintings that encircles the viewer.

Dadaism An anti-art movement started in 1915 that attempted to express the confusion and disorder of the world after World War I by rejecting traditional culture and ideas of beauty in art.

delineation The marking of the outlines of a form with clear, sharp lines.

draftsman A person who is skilled in the art of drawing.

excavate To dig out, or uncover, and remove. To make hollow by digging.

expressionism A movement in modern art that broke away from naturalism and distorted or exaggerated reality for emotional effect.

Fauves A group of early twentieth-century painters, led by the French painter Henri Matisse (1869–1954), who used vivid colors, flat patterns, and distorted forms. The word *fauve* means "wild beast" in French.

futurism A politically driven art movement that began in Italy in 1909. It glorified the modern world of machinery, speed, and violence.

Impressionism A nineteenth-century art movement that took a more spontaneous approach to painting, attempting to capture and portray the atmosphere of a given moment, usually identified by a strong concern for the changing qualities of light.

Industrial Revolution The period of social and technological change that occurred in the eighteenth century when agricultural nations became industrialized.

manifesto A public statement made by a person or group, outlining their actions and intentions.

mentor A teacher; an experienced and trusted advisor or counselor.

monarchy A form of government or state ruled by a king or queen.

myopia The inability to clearly see objects that are not close; nearsightedness.

Neoclassicism A European art movement of the late eighteenth and early nineteenth century that tried to re-create the classical style of ancient Greece and Rome.

neo-impressionism A late nineteenth-century movement in French painting that developed out of or reacted against Impressionism. The movement was concerned with the representation of light and color using a scientific approach to carefully construct compositions with the pointillism technique.

pioneer To originate or aid the early development of by leading or preparing the way for others to follow.

pointillism A technique, also known as divisionism, used by Neo-impressionists whereby a painting is made up of small dots of pure color that produce brilliant color effects when viewed from a distance.

realism In art, a movement that started in France in the mid-nineteenth century, the aim of which was to create accurate representations of reality.

Renaissance The cultural movement, originating in Italy during the fourteenth century and lasting until the seventeenth century, in which the art, literature, and ideas of ancient Greece were rediscovered and applied to the arts. The artistic style of this period.

retrospective exhibition An exhibition showing the work of a particular artist dating from the beginning to the end of his or her career.

surrealism An aesthetic movement of the 1920s and 1930s that attempted to portray thought, dreams, and the imagination.

truss A framework of beams or bars, usually arranged in a triangle, built to support a roof.

woodblock print A print made from a block of wood that has been carved with a design, inked, and then pressed against paper, also called a woodcut.

Index

Index